Like Shards of Glass

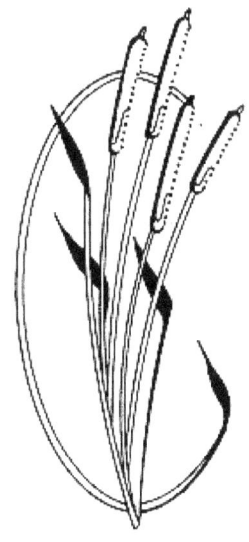

Like Shards of Glass

by Michael A. Budnik

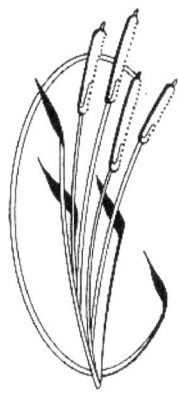

Editor

Mary E. Twomey
Johnathon D. Patterson

Senior Publisher
Steven Lawrence Hill Sr.

Awarded Publishing House
ASA Publishing Company

A Publisher Trademark Title page

ASA Publishing Company
Awarded Best Publisher for Quality Books
105 W. Front St., Suite 205, Monroe, Michigan 48161
www.asapublishingcompany.com

All Rights Reserved. No part of this publication may be reproduced, stored in a retrieval system or transmitted in any form or by any means electronic, mechanical, photocopying, recording or otherwise, without the prior written permission of the publisher. This book is a work of fictional reality and an instrument of opinionated liberty that is expounded and adhered to and within the boundaries of "1st Amendment" Freedom of Speech and the Legal Rights of the Constitution of the United States of America, and shall not be held with and against this freedom as due the Freedom of Conscience and Expression of Speech and/or Religion within the First Amendment.

      Any and all vending sales and distribution not permitted without full book cover and this title page.

Copyrights©2011 Michael A. Budnik, All Rights Reserved
Book: Like Shards of Glass
Date Published: 08.11 /Edition 2, Rev. 1
Trade Paperback, Book ID: ASAPCID2380574
ISBN: 978-1-886528-03-1
Library of Congress Cataloging-in-Publication Data

                This book was published in the United States of America.
                              State of Michigan

A Publisher Trademark Title page

Dedication

To my Mom and Dad
Sandra & Myron Budnik

Sister Nancy

Nephews and Nieces

Fred Shippy & Ray Gonzalez Gamboa Jr.

All the guys in the band
"Halloween"

Everyone in the band
"No Doubt"

Everyone at the Guitar Center
In Saginaw Michigan

Everyone at the "Peach Pit"
Restaurant

Everyone at Rite-Aid
In Saint Helen

Everyone at the
Regional Dialysis Center
In Westbranch Medical Center

and Special Thanks
to
Daniel Coffey

And Thanks to My ASA VIP Exclusive Team
Mary Twomey & Steven"LH" Sr.

Thanks!
Sincerely,
Michael A. Budnik

Like Shards of Glass

By Heavy Metal Musician

Michael A. Budnik

TABLE OF CONTENTS

Part One

Throwaways

The Sun Still Shines

Passing Fancies

Remedial Actions
Memorandum (R.A.M.)

Innocence Lost

As Was I

Father Ben

Love Affair

Quiet No More

Sudden Departures

Always Goodbye

Collective Bargaining

Part Two

You
Now all Your Dead Unknown

Power (F.T.N.)

Pain

Reachin' Thru the Mirror

Sharon

Sub Sunk

My Twisted Memories

Cards

Risk

Like Shards of Glass

Part Three

Just Pretend

Billy

Lighter Burns

No 911

Restricted Access

Encoding Error

End Game

Falling

Used Book

Part Four

Push-Pull Toy

I Must Insist

I Go Away

Survivors

Leave

Somethin'

Trust

Fuck off Asshole, (F.O.A.)

Stand Down

Letting Go

Make Friends with Pain

Part Five

That Place

Status Report

Comin' Back

For Bobby and Danny

Too Busy

Wet Paint

Safe Sex

Out There

Attorney Malpractice, (Thanks...Pris)

Sister Di

Bled Out

Michael A Budnik

Like Shards of Glass

Part Six

Starting Over

Sudden Deceleration Syndrome, (S.D.S.)

Numb

Denial

Beyond Redemption

Measured Response

Court Jester

Checkbook Justice

More to Follow

Without Warning

Like Shards of Glass

Part Seven

Dancer

To Love Again

Out With the Old

With Regret

No One

Outrage

Childs' Play

Wishing Well

Mikey's Dead

Play On

Michael A Budnik

Like Shards of Glass

Michael A Budnik

Like Shards of Glass

Part One

I mattered
Now shattered

Michael A Budnik

Like Shards of Glass

Throwaways

Just out of sight just out of mind
If you take time to be so kind
To see them fight to make their stand
You throw a dime and miss the grand
That is a risk you cannot take
For as they are you could be brand
With a walk brisk for your own sake
They fell so far these things you flee
You pass on by to your tower
They fade from sight with looks that plea
Each time they die adds your power
For them each night war comes, they find

See the hidden hear unbidden
Feel imperfect know their defect
Each time they try each time they cry
They are alone locked by stone
You want so much you want no such
You thank your luck you could be stuck
You want some love you seek your dove
You have no time you see no crime
What can they give? The price to live?
They have no one seen by no one
Hell that they save Hell yes they rave
Hell that they brave Hell yes they crave

They are alone cut to the bone
They see no one must be no one
so make some time and keep your dime
Come see them fight to stay in sight
keep them in mind and be so kind
Each time you try each time you cry
you can not fake for your own sake
too much at risk now with walk brisk
You thank your luck you could be stuck
Send them away keep them away
lock them away throw them away
throw them away Throw them away

Michael A Budnik

Like Shards of Glass

The Sun Still Shines

This life is fine
this way to find
The sun still shines
the ties still bind
A life was fine
a way to find
Old sun still shines
old lies still bind
No life is fine
no way to find
Your one still shines
your cries still bind

This life still yearns
this way to doom
The sun still churns
the ties still loom
A life still yearns
a way to bloom
Old sun still churns
old lies still gloom
No life that yearns
no way that doom
Your one still churns
your cries still boom

In the darkness
lessons learned
In the starkness
failure burned
Down in the void
worth nothing found
Pain to avoid
scream without sound
Just close your eyes
The sun still shines
These ties like lies
may just be binds

Life can be fine
The sun still shines
Those ties like lies
may just be binds
To keep your mind
Life will be fine
life will be fine
Those ties are lies
to keep your mind
The sun still shines
the sun still shines
the sun still shines

Michael A Budnik

Like Shards of Glass

Passing Fancies

Companionship
has sunk on me
All that friendship
lost in high seas
Feeling at bay
they went away
We were good friends
Before my fall
All those things end
It was their call
As I recall
was a long fall

While I want you
without knowing
I stay from you
without showing
You may see me
sunk in high seas
Without knowing
Without showing
As I recall
Before my fall
I mattered
Now shattered

There was a gem
Before my fall
Was one of them
expressive balls
First push, then shove
I was in love
Feeling at bay
I went away
Fearing some dread
inside I fled
As I recall
was a long fall

Michael A Budnik

Like Shards of Glass

Remedial Actions Memorandum (R.A.M.)

This happening
has no ending
Some names do change
with acts too strange
Belief banging
Relief hanging
Allow nations
their ambitions
This happening
Keeps happening
It will go on
and on and on

Charm does follow
harm grows hollow
Torture in bouts
future in doubts
Scorn by strangers
torn by dangers
Dust off lost screams
trust cost those dreams
Hope needs belief
cope needs relief
It will go on
and on and on

Need a job, dear
on your knees here
Go on and tell
welcome to hell
Torture in bouts
future in doubts
Dust off lost screams
trust cost those dreams
Allow nations
their ambitions
relieve banging
believe hanging

Michael A Budnik

Like Shards of Glass

Innocence Lost

In the darkness comes a madness
Without warning a gag quiets
that which has been waken in fear
A glint of steel in the moonlight
Followed by sharpness upon
a throat so intentions are clear
Between his chants off come the pants
There is dissent but no consent.
A child lives for another day
with hopes for a better someday
Survival is not revival
This fight is lost the war is not

Somewhere children play in the fields
nearby not knowing they need shields
One goes off with a person known
With the pain of betrayal still
burning throughout trust has been blown
Hell has just begun on that hill
While naked and tied to a tree
that child learns new ways of coping
with the rage and lets their mind free
This moment gives way to a hope
Better days are coming for me
This fight is lost the war is not

An annual camping trip gives
some animal an entire week
for stalking his helpless captive
This drama like rerun movies
plays out before an empty house
Exhaustion then devastation
No place left to escape the shame
Survival brings desperation
Enduring this rage burns a flame
This child learns new ways of coping
with the rage and lets their mind free
This war has cost innocence lost

Michael A Budnik

Like Shards of Glass

As Was I

Like dead and dying left rotten
They were left behind forgotten
The war was on no time to mourn
Thru chaos and fields left to burn
Time was at hand to make a stand
From the flames came an offensive
with the victory decisive
got away glad for just the day
The war was won it felt all done
Failed to know it just begun
Had too many losses to mourn
They were left behind as was I

Seems like a person caught in time
The body continued to grow
Feelings harmful and thus denied
To keep alive must analyze
Stay alert for those danger signs
If they are detected flee
Happened before now you see
Trust no one lessons learned
The war was won but never done
Had too many losses to mourn
Too many to face on my own
They were left behind as was I

Don't spend time on feeling sorrow
These are hellish themes to hear
Trust in someone from tomorrow
Put efforts where they need to be
On all your children of today
Listen to them Have time for them
Danger comes from those most trusted
Sometimes no matter what it happens
Listen to them believe in them
Don't let them face this hell alone
Don't leave them behind as was I
Like dead and dying left rotten

To be left behind forgotten
to be left behind forgotten
Like dead and dying left rotten
The war was won but never done
Have too many losses to mourn
too many to face on their own
To be left behind forgotten
to be left behind forgotten
to be left behind forgotten
Like dead and dying left rotten
To be left behind forgotten
to be left behind forgotten

Michael A Budnik

Like Shards of Glass

Father Ben

When I look back
the signs were there
This came apart
over some time
All I ever
wanted to have
All I ever
wanted to be
felt put at risk
From the inside
It began as
screams in the night

When they came back
All those nightmares
Woke with a start
in fear those times
All I ever
wanted to have
All I ever
wanted to be
was put at risk
No place to hide
All would be lost
No peace in sight

The more I tried
my life untied
I was alone
Fearing madness
feeling sadness
Mind shattered
life in tatters
This endless shame
carried my name
If they could see
they would leave me
I was at risk

No one would see
all the nothing
carried inside
No one would be
allowed inside
to know nothing
All I ever
wanted to have
All I ever
wanted to be
My life untied
the more I tried

Seems someone saw
I was taken
so a label
they could then make
All I ever
wanted to have
All I ever
wanted to be
Was lost that day
with the label
Been set apart
and thrown away

I am nothing
I have nothing
I see that now
but now I know
The shame and blame
not mine to bear
I leave to you
our Father Ben
those things you did
I remember
I was at risk
by what you did

Michael A Budnik

Like Shards of Glass

Love Affair

In my dreams I've held you
In my dreams I've touched you
In my dreams I've held you
In my dreams I've touched you
Then the day comes
and you you go away ^
to come again
another day ^

The days, they come
Just like my dreams
Yeah, it all seems just fine just fine
Oh drink a little bit of wine
In the mornin' I'll be just fine
Oh drink alittle bit of wine
In the mornin' I'll be just fine
Squeezin' my pillow so tightly ^

We pass on the
street you don't know
the love we share ^
My fantasy ^
I cannot dare
this love affair
My fallacy ^
Glad you can take this so lightly ^

Repeat 2 then 1

^ = Increase the volume

Michael A Budnik

Like Shards of Glass

Quiet No More

Shut the fuck up!
Not another
sound outta you
or I'll cut you
Do me right now
Just like before
I don't care if
it makes you sore
Don't fuck it up!
Do me right now!
Do me right now!
Do me right now!

Say a word to
anybody
They won't believe
a nobody
Do me right now
Take it up there
so what if it tears
I don't care if
it makes you sore
Do me right now!
Do me right now!
Do me right now!

If they find out
it's you sold out
You know it's wrong
Take it in there
Do me right now
You don't do that
I'll kill all those
you claim to love
Don't fuck it up!
Do me right now!
Do me right now!
Do me right now!

Years have gone by
Everything
that he had said
I believed
I can still hear
that kid in fear
Those scenes come by
but bring no peace
I don't care if
it makes you sore
I won't be kept
quiet no more!

Michael A Budnik

Like Shards of Glass

Sudden Departures

Anybody
Please, somebody
Can you hear me?
Anybody
Hey, somebody
You playin' me?
Anybody
Now somebody
Has to be there
Anybody
Be somebody
Please, I'm aware

Hello hello
I need someone
You said to call
Hello hello
Is there someone?
I'm gonna fall
Hello hello
Never someone
Too much to bear
Hello hello
Don't want someone
if they don't care

Excuse me God
Kept my promise
I said I'd call
Excuse me God
Owe no promise
As I recall
Excuse me God
Have no promise
They would not fail
Excuse me God
No more promise
Time to set sail

Michael A Budnik

Like Shards of Glass

Always Goodbye

Sittin' here now
Wonderin' 'bout
yesterday -
I know what you
want ---
I know what you
have to say -
It's the comin'
of the day -^
And I don't like
it! ---^^

The age we speak
The page we burn
You know, you know, you know
You have to have your fun
You never know
what the mornin'
will bring --^
Still I hear you
singin' --^^

Goodbye, goodbye
That's what you're singin' now
Goodbye goodbye
It's always the same song
Goodbye goodbye
That's what you let me know
Goodbye goodbye
It's always goodbye-
Always goodbye

Moments too soon
spent in wonder
Eternity
alone now -
I would sell my
soul and all my
tomorrows -
for a moment of
yesterday -^

Goodbye, goodbye
That's what you tell me now
Goodbye, goodbye
It's always the same song
Goodbye, goodbye
It's always the same -
Always goodbye

Hello --
is always followed
by goodbye -
Always Goodbye

And now --
the truth I found
It's always too late
it's always the same

Hello --
is always followed
by goodbye -
Always goodbye ^
Always goodbye ^^
Always goodbye ^^^
Always goodbye ^^^^
It's always goodbye
Always goodbye ^
It's always goodbye
Always goodbye ^^
Always goodbye ^
Always goodbye ^^

^ = Increase the volume
- = Hold for a beat

Michael A Budnik

Like Shards of Glass

Collective Bargaining

Look at the face
  not of this place
Fearing attack
  Just staring back
from the mirror
  Spares the terror
that pain reflects
  from sight deflects
Disconnected
  Reconnected
The two must be
  for them to be

Look at the face
  before this space
It is safe here
  nothing to fear
See the mirror
  and the error
See no reject
  See no object
Painful feeling
  sent you reeling
With you along
  you do belong

Look at your face
  More than a case
in the mirror
  Part the mirror
Let go your hate
  open your gate
There may be fear
  from past not near
Your suppression
  brings depression
With you along
  you do belong

Look at my face
  I hate this place
If I let go
  Pain-in-the-ass
bitch in flat glass
  I let me go
Too much was lost
  too high the cost
All I am died
  nothing inside
With me along
  never belong

Disconnected
  Reconnected
The two must be
  for you to be
This suppression
  feeds depression
With you along
  you do belong
With you along
  you can belong
With you along
  you will belong

With you along
  we can belong
With you along
  we do belong
With you along
  we will belong
With you along
  we can belong
With you along
  we do belong
With you along
  we will belong

Michael A Budnik

Like Shards of Glass

Michael A Budnik

Like Shards of Glass

Part Two

I shed so many tears
I bled so many years
I fed so many fears

Michael A Budnik

Like Shards of Glass

You

"I want you" the "man" says
"See the world join us now"
Just the seas "he" won't say
"He" wants you don't care how
Your nation comes to call
Your station first to fall
"We give you" gives you shits
"We need you" take the hits
That's the job lives to rob
"All" at stake kills to make
Impact you compact you
Mislay you betray you

"Learn as you earn"
Burn as you churn
Raise the carrots
They need parrots
to use so they
abuse their prey
For your nation
stay your station
All your hopes lost
all their hopes frost
Answer the call
and you will fall

"Not just a job" is just a job
Your will it chokes you're ill no
jokes
Stay your station they mislay you
Stay your nation they betray you
then subtract you then detract you
Recall the pact they stall the pact
raise the carrots they need parrots
they can abuse they need to use
Answer the call and you will fall
they mislay you they betray you
Answer the call and you will fall
Answer the call and you will fall

Michael A Budnik

Like Shards of Glass

Now All Your Dead Unknown

Sign up everyone
Yes women come along
They want to throw
your life away
Sing me your death march song
You got no chance to grow
Your will is what they say
Come now everyone
Live unknown die unknown
Now all your dead unknown
Your hope has just been blown
Now all your dead unknown

They claim the will you sold
You maim and kill as told
in fields full of flowers
no shields stop fire powers
Your skill is what they say
that hill they want this day
Sing me your death watch song
You got no chance to sow
Live unknown die unknown
Now all your dead unknown
Your hope is not your own
Now all your dead unknown

Go on everyone
Hey women come along
They have to throw
your life away
This is your death watch song
You lost your chance to know
Your fill is what they say
As kill you are this day
Live unknown die unknown
Now all your dead unknown
Your hope you cost as shown
Now all your dead unknown

Michael A Budnik

Like Shards of Glass

Power (F.T.N.)

You have to know it won't be kind
But you do show you must be blind
With no outrage you give "okay"
with your blank page they have your say
You must not hear you must not care
they live in fear that they can't dare
Those they "must" trust have all the say
to use that "must" to have their way
Just an escape getting their due
Some may say "rape" that may be true
Power to use those in their charge
Power abuse by those in charge

Do on demand Chain of Command
Nothing to say they have all say
You make a claim and they take aim
No way you pay their way all day
When it's over they discover
Personality Disorder
They claim you had too bad so sad
So take a bow can't use you now
Your mind "they find" disordered
Rape is okay do as they say
Power to use those in their charge
Power abuse by those in charge

Some live today hope for the day
those they "must" trust will use that "must"
just for the job not hope to rob
To some hope cost today is lost
now so are they their hopes were prey
You take your aim they make a claim
no way to win that was your sin
Getting their due was wrong untrue
What you call rape just an escape
You pay their way all day they say
Power to use those in their charge
Power abuse by those in charge

Michael A Budnik

Like Shards of Glass

Pain

I've come for you fate claims it's due
I come as rage hate burns your page
You dug this grave so now be brave
For you no deal I do not feel
Those souls impact a pact intact
Know me I'm pain you I disdain
From all the tears and all the fears
those you ordain fear me I'm pain
Those souls impact now act intact
Pain comes for you pain calls for you
So now be brave you dug your grave
Hate burns your page it becomes rage

Pain is now near now you know fear
Run if you will fate claims its fill
You are cancer have no answer
Lost souls demand you take the stand
Admit your wrongs you must be strong
Your soul you save you must be brave
From all the fears and all the tears
those you ordain see me I'm pain
You dug this grave you must be brave
Those souls impact now rest our pact
Feel me I'm pain peace you now gain
Rest now in peace I'm pain all pain

Feel me your pain
Know me your pain
Must use your pain
Don't fear your pain
Don't lose your pain
Don't cause your pain
Don't pause your pain
PAIN
PAIN
PAIN
Feel me your pain
Know me your pain

Michael A Budnik

Like Shards of Glass

Reachin' Thru the Mirror

Out of thin air
so fine and fair
As some magic
just as tragic
Over before
it had begun
So far from shore
Far from the sun
Those days are gone
Long to belong
Fears cost ourselves
Tears lost ourselves

Reachin' thru the mirror
I'll take what I can find
Reachin' thru the mirror
I'll take what I can mind

Long to belong
Those days are gone
In rage I find
My cage I mind
Fears lost ourselves
Tears cost ourselves
Like some tragic
act of magic
Over before
it begun
So far from shore
Far from the sun

Reachin' thru the mirror
I'll take what I can find
Reachin' thru the mirror
I'll take what I can mind

Reachin' thru the mirror
Long to belong with you
Reachin' thru the mirror
There's nothin' I can do
Reachin' thru the mirror

Reachin' thru the mirror ^
Reachin' thru the mirror ^^
Reachin' thru the mirror ^^^
Reachin' thru the mirror ^^^^

^ = Increase the volume

Michael A Budnik

Like Shards of Glass

Sharon (Aron - if female singer)

Please tell me how I can go on
without you now I miss you so
If you see me I love you oh
If you hear me now my Sharon
I'm so sorry I let you down
You must worry as I go down
this path alone within without
without no tone lost in this doubt

Tease me okay but please I'm lost
no words can say the hell I've cost
As I go down I let you down
I'm so sorry that you worry
I miss you so I love you oh
I don't know how I can go on
without you now now my Sharon

Tease me okay please there's no way
that I know how to go on now
Without you years have gone in tears
I'm so sorry that I let you down
You must worry as I go down
I'm so sorry that you worry
I miss you so I love you oh
I will go on for you Sharon

Michael A Budnik

Like Shards of Glass

Sub Sunk

All stations attention
Uncontrolled flooding
in emotion section
Too much feeling flooding
Critical condition
Send out our position
Tell them the boat's goin' down
be lost without a sound

Energy production
Failing on relation
Uncontrolled flooding
in emotion section
Too much feeling flooding
Critical condition
Send out our position
Now failing all stations

Critical condition
Send out our position
Uncontrolled flooding
in emotion section
Too much feeling flooding
All stations attention
Now failing all stations
Abandon all stations

Michael A Budnik

Like Shards of Glass

My Twisted Memories

You ain't shit take the hit
take the hit you ain't shit
You should die wish you'd try
wish you'd try you should die
Make it stop let it drop
let it drop make it stop
I'll be good know I should
know I should I'll be good
Just as bad just like Dad
just like Dad just as bad

Internal
Eternal
My twisted memories
Failing recoveries

Take the hit you ain't shit
you ain't shit take the hit
Wish you'd die you should try
you should try wish you'd die
Let it drop make it stop
make it stop let it drop
Know I should I'll be good
I'll be good know I should
Just like Dad just as bad
just as bad just like Dad

Internal
Eternal
My twisted memories
Failing recoveries

My twisted memories
Failing discoveries
My twisted memories
My twisted memories
My twisted memories
My twisted memories

Michael A Budnik

Like Shards of Glass

Cards

So from these shards been dealt these cards
some good some bad none can be had
Don't play don't fly keep them close by
Like a mother wren by her nest
I keep my cards close to my vest
Not mine to choose just mine to lose
All I do wrong I've lived that song
So high the stakes no plays to make

I still have these cards in my hand
to stay or fold or make my stand
Like a mother wren by her nest
I keep my cards close to my vest
Not mine to choose just mine to lose
There has to be more than I see
Don't play don't try don't stay don't fly
So high the stakes find plays to make

These are my cards dealt from these shards
some good some bad some can be had
So stay or fold or make your stand
I still have these cards in my hand
Not mine to choose just yours to lose
There has to be more than I see
Don't play don't try don't stay don't fly
So high the stakes got plays to make

Michael A Budnik

Like Shards of Glass

Risk

Foolish again tisk tisk
Reached out took a risk
By now should know better
now waiting for letter
All good things pass on me
You watch just wait you'll see

I shed too many tears
I bled too many years
I fed too many fears

Postman across the way
the word is due today
By now should know better
Here it is the letter
Can't be you love me too
It says you love me too

I shed so many tears
I bled so many years
I fed so many fears

See it here says it here
You love me you love me
It can't be it can be
You love me you love me
You love me you love me
You love me you love me

Michael A Budnik

Like Shards of Glass

Michael A Budnik

Like Shards of Glass

Part Three

I know you will leave me alone
My dues paid not enough for you

Michael A Budnik

Just Pretend

So you think I don't know
that I don't have a clue
While I try not to show
that I know you're untrue
Though my heart is breaking
and our world is quaking
I see this as an end
my heart must now defend
I don't want us to end
so now I just pretend
I know you just pretend
Look how we just pretend

This could be a mistake
I think not and feel sad
All we have is at stake
I go on and feel mad
Though our hearts are breaking
and our worlds are quaking
This must be at an end
our hearts must now defend
We don't want us to end
so now we just pretend
We know we just pretend
Look how we just pretend

Though our hearts are breaking
and our worlds are quaking
This must be at an end
our hearts must now defend
We don't want us to end
so now we just pretend
Guard our hearts to the end
we know we just pretend
Guard our hearts to the end
look how we just pretend
What we have just pretend
What we have just pretend

Michael A Budnik

Like Shards of Glass

Billy

Now Billy how silly
Got caught with your pants down
You're too old still class clown
Oh Billy so silly
No one believes you now
Just you deceives you now

Now Billy how silly
Broke our trust go you must
You tell lies you sell cries
Oh Billy so silly
Just you deceives you now
No one believes you now

Oh Billy so silly
Oh Billy go Billy
Go Billy go Billy
Go go go Billy go
So silly go Billy

Now Billy how silly
You think above it all
We think about to fall
Oh Billy so silly
No one believes you now
Just you deceives you now

Oh Billy so silly
Oh Billy go Billy
Go Billy go Billy
Go go go Billy go
So silly go Billy

Oh Hilly so silly
Oh Hilly go Hilly
Go Hilly go Hilly
Go go go Hilly go
So silly go Hilly

So silly Oh Billy

Michael A Budnik

Like Shards of Glass

Lighter Burns

Flick flick flick on the bic
Burning flesh makes me sick
need the pain to stay here
Footsteps comin' now near
We have been here before
so we know what's in store
Too much too soon too late
So clutch so boon so hate
This far and no farther
Lighter burns on farther
lighter burns on farther
lighter burns on farther

Tic tic tic goes the bic
Flames to life on oil slick
need the flame to stay here
Flame is his biggest fear
We have been here before
so we know what's in store
Too much too soon too late
So clutch so boon so hate
This far and no farther
Lighter burns go farther
lighter burns go farther
lighter burns go farther

The flame grows his fear shows
The chase is on and on
Gunfire from him strikes near
Long before lost that fear
We just hide in the smoke
and wait and wait for now
our time to strike and strike
Never ever touch me
This far and no farther
Lighter burns no farther
lighter burns no farther
lighter burns no farther

Michael A Budnik

Like Shards of Glass

No 911

You hear it on the news
see it in the papers
The bad cops stain the blues
with their crimes and capers
No way to tell the good
from bad those that are hoods

If help I need
would rather bleed
No 911
Have my own gun
No 911
Won't be their fun

Call for aid if you've paid
those on the take
Could be a fake
Help comes late they claim fate
No way to tell the good
from bad those that are hoods

If help I need
would rather bleed
No 911

Have my own gun
No 911
Won't be their fun
No 911
So sad bad one
No 911
Over now done

Michael A Budnik

Like Shards of Glass

Restricted Access

I'm not asking you to believe
that seems too much for me to ask
It'd be nice if pain you'd relieve
that seems too much for me to ask
You claim I need to pay my dues
I need to let my feelings show
If you'd look you'd see I've left clues
that dues were paid no more I owe
To regain access to feeling
have to blast thru defense reeling
Reach that place shut down so alone
Feelings flooding in I'm alone

I'm not asking you to receive
that seems too much for me to ask
It'd be nice if you'd not deceive
that seems too much for me to ask
Uncontrolled feelings flooding
You want my feelings to be shown
I feel anger burn in my blood
now that my defense has been blown
I know you will leave me alone
My dues paid not enough for you
Must deny access feel alone
Feelings flooding in I'm alone

Michael A Budnik

Like Shards of Glass

You want my feelings to be shown
now that my defense has been blown
Just hold me some feel so alone
I know you will leave me alone
You want my feelings to be shown
now that my defense has been blown
Please hold me some feel so alone
I know you will leave me alone
Now that my defense has been blown
you want my feelings to be shown
Please hold me some feel so alone
I know you will leave me alone

Michael A Budnik

Like Shards of Glass

Encoding Error

Don't you touch me that might free me
You are too near too much I fear
I long so much long for you much
I am never nor forever
Too much lost time to heal their crime
too much to spend on me to mend
It is my turn for me to burn
So to lost friends I seek my end
Gone for my mode now there's no code

Don't you touch me that could free me
I can't tell kind from hell's unkind
Don't care for me rage burns in me
Too afraid to let you come near
I am never nor forever
Too much lost time to heal their crime
too much to spend on me to mend
So to lost friends I seek my end
Gone for my mode now there's no code

Don't look for me best not to see
the mess inside I've tried to hide
Don't you touch me don't trust touch see
I can't tell kind from hell's unkind
I am never nor forever
Too much lost time to heal their crime
too much to spend on me to mend
So to lost friends I seek my end
Gone for my mode now there's no code

Michael A Budnik

Like Shards of Glass

End Game

You save yourself to save yourself
You gave them names to hide your shames
Now cave to blames and ride the flames
Wish to send same you call end game

To you those names just names
You shift blame for no blame
Hide your shames ride the flames
Call end game all end game

A mean to an end
A clean slate to mend
Cave to blames in flames
To send same end game

Must save yourself just save yourself
You gave them names to hide your shames
Now cave to blames and ride the flames
Wish to send same you call end game

Must save just save yourself
Those names our names you gave
Hide shames ride flames we rave
To mend our end end game

Michael A Budnik

Falling

If I should die without a cry
before my time bury me with
with my little dictionary
As close as I'll ever come to
have my dream mate or my dream
state
I am falling my way to hell
but I've missed I'm so pissed
No more stalling leave this my shell
but I've missed I'm so pissed
Look what I fell into falling
on thru nightmares I'm recalling
Look what I fell into calling

My dream love is now my love
I've been falling my way to hell
but I've missed was so pissed
Now I'm calling from this my shell
so I've missed was so pissed
Look what I fell into calling
into daydreams I'm recalling
Look what I fell into falling
Now all my dreams I hear calling
hear them clearly feel so nearly
My dreams calling I am falling
I was falling as dreams calling

In love falling now love calling
So now look what I fell into
All my hopes and dreams I'm into
I am falling my love calling

In love falling now love calling
So now look what I fell into
All my hopes and dreams I'm into
I am falling my love calling

In love falling now love calling
So now look what I fell into
All my hopes and dreams I'm into
I am falling my love calling

Like Shards of Glass

Used Book

All my pages are worn and fray
some have pieces missin' torn 'way
I was once a classic novel
Fallen now just this used book
I don't deserve a second book

I have art added to my pages
they too have faded from the ages
Many tell of some Jan Marie
I guess she gave good head for fee
I recall she read my novel

I was once a classic novel
Fallen now just this used book
I don't deserve a second look
Please won't someone throw me away
all my pages are worn and fray

Someone comin' oh please not now
It's Jan Marie throw me away
She knows my once-classic novel
Ever more than this used book
She's takin' this used book home

Michael A Budnik

Like Shards of Glass

Michael A Budnik

Like Shards of Glass

Part Four

I know a friend of yours
I know what your heart stores

Michael A Budnik

Like Shards of Glass

Push-Pull Toy

I live in fear that some may hear
the shame I hide am lost inside
Don't like it here I won't stay here
You are too near and not too near
I want you near and hate my fear
So go away now go away
I don't know what you want today
I don't know what you want to stay
So go away now go away
I don't know how to let you near
I don't know how to shake this fear
So go away now go away

I feel like a kill-joy
You must feel just like my
Push-Pull Toy Push-Pull Toy
I am such a kill-joy
You must think you are a
Push-Pull Toy Push-Pull Toy

I won't stay here don't like it here
You are too near and not too near
I want you near and hate my fear
So go away now go away
I don't have what you want today
I don't have what you want to stay
So go away now go away
I don't know how to let you know
I don't know how to let you go
So go away now go away
So go away now go away
So go away now go away

Repeat second part and end

Michael A Budnik

I Must Insist

It's all my fault
I must insist
Not the adult
I must resist
Take blame take shame
I just exist

If I take blame
take their power
If I take shame
stake their tower
I must resist
I just exist

It's all my fault
I just insist
Not you adult
I just resist
Take blame take shame
I must exist

If it's your fault
I can't insist
Must trust adult
I can't resist
Your blame your shame
I can't exist

So now you see
I must insist
For me to be
I must resist
It must be me
I must exist

There is no trust
I must insist
All that is dust
I must resist
Stay in tower
I must exist
Stay in power
I must insist

So now you see
I must exist
For me to be
I must resist
It must be me
I must insist

Like Shards of Glass

Go Away

I can barely hear you as I
now slip away gone for this day
While you're barely before my eyes
You ache today more than you say
I slip away I go away
Right here before your eyes no score
I slip away I go away
As I never leave "here" ever

Need you to stay need you to say
that you love me and let me be
I'm so afraid hell from past raid
Please just hold me it's got hold me
I slip away I go away
Right here before your eyes no score
I slip away I go away
As I never leave "here" ever

All this is new don't have a clue
You ache today more than you say
Need you to stay need you to say
that you love me and let me be
I slip away I go away
I'm so afraid hell from past raid
Please just hold me it's got hold me
I slip away I go away
Right here before your eyes no score
I slip way I go way
As I never leave "here" ever
I slip away I go away

Michael A Budnik

Like Shards of Glass

Survivors

Been such a long time
since this seen as crime
If once you've been had
that's twice you've been sad
Been such a long time
since we had our time
Still we don't know why
or when time to cry
Just know we go on
Wipe away the tears
and we just go on
Lie away the fears
so we just go on
Been such a long time
left behind in sight
too small for a fight

If once you've been had
that's twice you've been sad
Just know we go on
Wipe away the tears
and we just go on
Lie away the fears
So we just go on
So we just go on

Been such a long time
as this been seen crime?
If once you've been had
that's twice you've been sad
Been such a long time
since we had our time
Still we don't know why
or when time to cry
Just know we go on
Wipe away the tears
and we just go on
Lie away the fears
So we just go on
Been such a long time
left behind in sight
too small for a fight

If once you've been had
that's twice you've been sad
Just know we go on
Wipe away the tears
and we just go on
Lie away the fears
So we just go on
so we just go on

Michael A Budnik

Like Shards of Glass

Leave

I want to give myself to you
show you how my love grows for you
When I'm with you feel like brand new
I don't know how to show you how
this feels inside no need to hide

All that I am want to give you
show you how my love grows for you
This is brand new don't have a clue
I see it like it went before
won't put you thru that hell in store

Bein' here stayin' here takes more
showing you knowing you scrams core
I want you ways that can't be scored
But I want you and I see you
then I can see me hurting you

You can't see the hell I live with
So I ask you to go 'way with
someone other than I just "leave"
Forget about all the rest "leave"
I see it now so go please "leave"

Michael A Budnik

Like Shards of Glass

Somethin'

You see somethin' here that calls you
You want somethin' near that calls you
Don't care somethin' here could mall you
don't care somethin' near may hall you

That somethin' been here for ages
that somethin' calls now and rages
Somethin' only knows it refires
somethin' only grows in desires

Somethin' now knows it longs for you
somethin' opens its gate for you
Now it's up to you to teach it love
now it's up to you reach with love

Once it bears its heart to the you
you must stay and see its way thru
Show it compassion for others
show your passion for this somethin'

Now it's up to you to teach it love
now it's up to you reach with love
Somethin' now knows it longs for you
somethin' opens its gate for you

Show your passion for this somethin'

Michael A Budnik

Trust

I see you look at me
you get so curious
As you get far from me
I see you look at me
you get so furious
Then you get far from me

I know a friend of yours
I know what your heart stores
They told you to hold to
you're known to fly unknown
You see charm turn to harm
All you've known all they've shown

Please take my hand
trust is learned
I understand
trust is earned

I see you look at me
you are so curious
Please stay here let's be near
I see you look at me
and feel so curious
Please stay here let's be near

I understand
trust is learned
Please take my hand
trust is earned

Let me earn yours
behind closed doors
Let me learn yours
behind closed doors
Let me earn yours
Let me learn yours

Like Shards of Glass

Fuck Off Asshole, (F.O.A.)

Must have made a mistake
I'm the wrong side of right
Feels like I'm put to stake
That's some might for the right
As I burn I must say
You let me burn this way
Free my rage from this cage
as my page leaves this age
Now don't you make a mistake
fall to the wrong side of right
Know the score fell before
I forgave now I rave

Must be might makes you right
"Just" lost sight lost from light
My mistake mine to make
yours to take gone for sake
I'm the wrong side of right
You're the strong side of might
That's just how these things are
too bad now gone too far
Now don't you make mistake
fall to the wrong side of right
Know the score fell before
I forgave now I rave

Must have made big mistake
I'm the wrong side of right
and now I'm put to stake
That's some might for the right
So I'll burn for you pay
You let me burn this way
Free my rage from this cage
so my page leaves this age
From my grave I will rave
That's just how these things are
too bad now gone too far
From my grave I will rave

Michael A Budnik

Like Shards of Glass

Stand Down

Don't come to me
in your times of
manned troubles
Don't ask me to
recall good times
there's just troubles

You left me behind
you hope I don't mind
after the harm you cause
You hope my heart will pause
before I respond in kind
Now is your chance Stand Down

Don't come to me
in your times of
planned troubles
Don't ask me to
recall good times
there's just troubles

You hope I don't mind
you left me behind
You hope my heart will pause
after the harm you cause
Now is your chance to stand down
before I respond in kind

Now you pray I'll Stand Down
For hell you gave Stand Down
Now you say you'll Stand Down
I'll respond now.............
I won't Stand Down...........

Michael A Budnik

Letting Go

I just won't care that's my hell bare
Open my heart torn from the start
Repeat mistake burn at the stake
I've tried to reach tried and lost each
I just don't care to hell with dare
Time to let go my dreams clung to
So long to those hopes I hung to
Nothin' more to hold this life to

I just won't care all my hell bare
Repeat mistake burn at the stake
I've tried to reach hope beyond reach
Keep out my heart deep cut from start
I just don't care to hell with dare
Time to let go my dreams clung to
So long to those hopes I hung to
Nothin' more to hold this life to

I just don't care that's my hell bare
Repeat mistake burn at the stake
I've tried to reach hope beyond reach
Keep out my heart deep cut from start
I just don't care to hell with dare
Time to let go my dreams clung to
So long to those hopes I hung to
Nothin' more to hold this life to

Like Shards of Glass

Make Friends with Pain

At the end of my rope
Stuck out here in the rain
Need to let go my hope
Just to make friends with pain

Been fighting to get by
Life sighting was the rope
Now it seems just a lie
Need to let go my hope

Nothing remains
Make friends with pain
So let it rain
Make friends with pain

Today was tomorrow
only just yesterday
Leads to other sorrows
When it's done all you say

Nothing remains
Make friends with pain
So let it rain
Make friends with pain

At the end of my rope
Need to let go my hope
Just let it rain
Make friends with pain
Nothing remains
Make friends with pain
Make friends with pain
Make friends with pain

Michael A Budnik

Like Shards of Glass

Part Five

I've been down the path you walk now
I wish I could tell you all's well

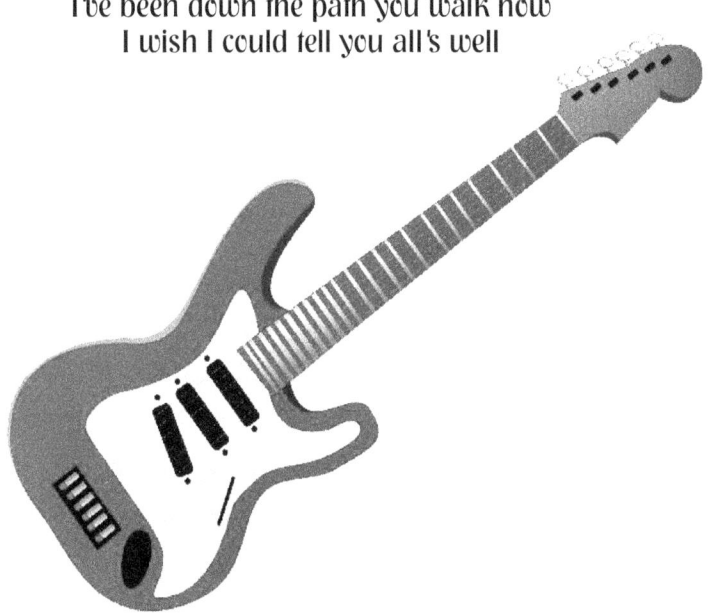

Michael A Budnik

That Place

Takes just seconds for discrimination
then they must make their
recrimination
Some memorial so raptorial
Those presidential claim preferential
You been bought now feel
overwrought
You in your buff I must rebuff
Destination determination
discrimination recrimination
There must be a place that just
shows
there must be a place that just knows
There is no place for discrimination
then no need to seed recrimination

This inquisition needs inhibition

It's such a shame that place not here
so place no blame no space not here
Though that place is in range
target trace can make change
Too safe to hate
not leave to fate
So have a hand go make your stand
All the lost time lost to this crime
There must be a place that just grows
there must be a place that just shows
There is no place for discrimination
then no need to seed recrimination

This inquisition needs inhibition

You in your buff I must rebuff
You been bought now feel
overwrought
It's such a shame our place not here
no place no blame no space not here
Though that place is in range
target trace can make change
So memorial too raptorial
Those presidential claim preferential
There must be a place that just grows
there must be a place that just knows
There is no place for discrimination
then no need to seed recrimination

Like Shards of Glass

Status Report

Those that can do
Those that can't do it too play teach
Those that want you to do say rules
they stay above
Those that can't do but want their ass
kissed too play preach
Those that are left to just make do
must give way
and some say they must pay each
We face this place that is not ours in
space
Though those above claim we have
here our place
Our vote is just a tote
Their vote like a remote they tote like
a garrote

Such a shame what stays same us to
blame ours in name

This is our way seems just their way
Our place to pay their place to say
Not too nice here too much vice here
They set aside the rules we bide as
they may hide
Out in plain view none may review
They claim guilt without due process
Then maim innocence in name of
progress
Our vote is just a tote
Their vote like a remote they tote like
a garrote

Such a shame what stays same us to
blame ours in name

Those that can do
Those that can't do it too play teach
Those that want you to do say rules
they stay above
Those that can't do but want their ass
kissed too play preach
Those that are left to just make do
must make way
And some say they must pay each
They set aside the rules we bide as
they may hide
Out in plain view none may review
Our vote is just a tote
Their note like a remote they tote like
a garrote

Such a shame what stays same us to
blame ours in name

Michael A Budnik

Like Shards of Glass

Comin' Back

I've been down the path you walk now
I wish I could tell you all's well
Things for you have gone all to hell
Your life as you know it over
Must make a turn and not return

You want to go back
before the attack
Show them all is well
They want the you from
time before you fell
and that you is gone
That you has a cost
New you comes with dawn

I've been down the path you walk now
I wish I could tell you all's well
Things for you have gone all to hell
Your life as you know it over
Must make a turn and not return

I went on back there
to all those blank stares
I had to show them
that it all was well
What came back was not
what they would choose well
That me now is gone
New me came with dawn

I've been down the path you walk now
I wish I could tell you all's well
Things for you have gone all to hell
Your life as you know it over
Must make a turn and not return
things for you will go all to hell
Must make a turn and not return
down this path all you'll find is pain
Must make a turn and not return
must make a turn and not return

Michael A Budnik

Like Shards of Glass

For Bobby and Danny

I know this can't make up for all
of my many many shortfalls
I know I don't say I love you
as much as you both need to hear
It has nothing to do with you
It's just my fear I hold you dear
No matter what I say this loud
no matter what you make me proud
No matter what I play this loud
no matter what you make me proud

I don't want you to be like me
there's a world here for you to see
Need to prepare and take the dare
I love you both don't look to me
I hold you dear don't be like me
It's just my fears might hear my tears
No matter what I say this loud
no matter what you make me proud
No matter what I play this loud
no matter what you make me proud

This path I face hollow
I ask you not follow
No math to check my sums
Your task has yet to come
Let it rain treats oh yum
Even Cookie gets some
No matter what I say this loud
no matter what you make me proud
No matter what I play this loud
no matter what you make me proud

Michael A Budnik

Like Shards of Glass

Too Busy

You don't know this
too much amiss
You have no care
too much to bear
So much to do
too much for you
Time keeps moving
too much proving
Feel like a thief
too much too brief
You have no clue
too much all due

You don't know me
too much I see
Though once you did
too much I bid
You have a dime
too much no time
Don't seem to hear
too much lost dear
Won't be reached
too much breached
You just lost me
too much cost me

You don't hear me
too much dear fee
You don't know this
too much amiss
You don't know me
too much I see
You have no care
too much to bear
You just lost me
too much cost me
You have no clue
too much all due

Michael A Budnik

Wet Paint

This big sign says "Live Nude Dancing"
was so sure just active prancing
I should have known I would be shown
As I came in the door
this naked woman smiles
Bet she thought I would hit the floor
She then tells me "Beware wet paint"
Swear she must be some kind of saint
Her bounce so nice no vice
Take care I just may faint
beware don't touch wet paint
Afraid I just may faint
beware don't touch wet paint
beware don't touch wet paint

Then this dancer just in wet paint
takes my hand leads me to my stand
Music erupts from this huge stage
all these women breakin' out cage
As I stood there before the stage
This woman smiles then she rips cord
So much water no more wet paint
just so much wet bouncin' so nice
Please be my pet raid county vice
Take care I just may faint
beware don't touch wet paint
Afraid I just may faint
there goes my would-be saint
beware don't touch wet paint

Like Shards of Glass

They took her 'way left me to stay
I had my bail must thought must sail
Such a pity uptight city
I should have known I would be shown
be left all wet and with no pet
Still takin' 'way my wayward saint
all that bouncin' so nice no vice
Afraid I just may faint
raid ended show too soon
Beware don't touch wet paint
beware don't touch wet paint
beware don't touch wet paint
There goes my would-be saint
beware don't touch wet paint

Michael A Budnik

Safe Sex

I wanna take Vanna shake Vanna
Oh Vanna flies my kite trips my light
She's a sight bet she's tight fucks all night
Whips and chains loves the rain rocks off pain

I wanna shake Vanna take Vanna
Oh Vanna blows ram drive slows jam dive
She's a sight bet she's tight fucks all night
Whips and chains comes in rain jacks off pain

Gimmee Vanna gimmee Vanna
Oh please Vanna now please Vanna
Do me Vanna do me Vanna
Don't tease Vanna oh please Vanna
Suck me Vanna fuck me Vanna
Suck me Vanna fuck me Vanna

Repeat first 3 groups

Will never be ever
So clever this never
Forever will sever this one
Two never be ever as one
Know no one that I can let near
When they come near so much I fear
So I pretend
must try to mend
Someday they say
one day I may

Like Shards of Glass

Out There

There are times when one must take
stock
we must face our memory block
some may say ignore future shock
Blow the doors wide
face that inside
place that outside
I must face them alone
with just this heart of stone
I hear them say "no tone"
I was left here
left in some sphere
want to leave here

I was left by the flock
with my memory block
alone future shock
Naked doors wide
deep from inside
keep from outside
I won't face them alone
must crush this heart of stone
alone I am "no tone"
They left me here
left in some sphere
must leave "this" here

My heart not stone out there
my mind alone out there
won't find my tone out there
don't mind alone out there

I know my place out there
I know my space out there
Lost my time cost my time
Not my place nor my space
I belong now out there
now belong with out there
Too long tried to belong
so long died to belong
I belong now out there
now belong with out there
Your place unkind my place my
mind

My heart not stone out there
my mind alone out there
won't find my tone out there
don't mind alone out there
Not stone out there
my tone out there
alone out there
out there
out there
there

Michael A Budnik

Like Shards of Glass

Attorney Malpractice, (Thanks...Pris)

Trusted you with my stand
busted to hell by your hand
Pris let the statute run
Pris done before begun
Call that "free legal aid"
ball-bat me - legal laid

Pris you cost my last stand
Pris you lost my last strand
Too busy for this fight
too dizzy more on sight
All that "free legal aid"
stall that fee legal laid

Pris you took a sure win
with your hook left pure sin
Trusted you with my stand
busted to hell by your hand
Pris you lost my last stand
Pris you cost my last strand
All that "free legal aid"
ball-bat me - legal laid

Michael A Budnik

Like Shards of Glass

Sister Di

I hope you have found peace
for you your death release
I think you must have known
you let my hopes be blown
Sister Di by saying that nothing
let him keep saying I was nothing
He's been long gone so long
but what was done stays here way too long

For me I know no peace
those good times no release
You did all that nothing
let him and did nothing
I think you must have known
you let my dreams be blown
He's been long gone so long
but what was done stays here way too long

Sister Di I will not forgive you
will do what I must to forget you
You did all that nothing
let him and did nothing
I know you must have known
you let my dreams be blown
He's been long gone so long
but what was done stays here way too long

Michael A Budnik

Bled Out

With each word passing more of me bled out
while time keeps passing need much more red out
Feels like so much dead out
Like none of this read out
So opened those parts long forgotten
seems like you feel I just belong rotten
Opened my heart over right from the start
now I feel must be time to just depart

While time keeps passing more of me bled out
with each word passing need much more red out
Like none of this read out
Feels like too much dead out
Must close those parts so long rotten
Seems like some feel I belong forgotten
Opened my heart over right from the start
now I feel must be time to just depart

With each word passing more of me fled out
while time keeps passing so much more bled out
Feels like all this dead out
Like none of this read out
Must close those parts so long rotten
seems like I feel I belong forgotten
Opened my heart over right from the start
now I feel must be time to just depart

Like Shards of Glass

Michael A Budnik

Like Shards of Glass

Part Six

"The more I recall those lost times before my fall
The more I know more I just want to lose it all"

Michael A Budnik

Starting Over

Here I am stuck back in this place
Have no reason
to be in this unkind bad space
Just this season
at least that's what he claims
Run East as he takes aim
Just a bad memory
Like some sad history
Gimmee reason
not more treason
To start again been just an end
Have no reason just this season keep
that treason

So much time must have lapsed
since last time I collapsed
Fear I won't know myself
Fear I won't show myself
Here I am stuck back in this space
Have no reason
to be in this unkind bad place
Just this season
Like some sad history
Just a bad memory
Gimmee reason not more treason
to start again been just an end
Have no reason just this season keep
that treason

See no reason for his treason
I know I'm more than this
See no reason for his treason
I know will know no bliss
Gimmee reason not more treason
to be again for me again
Fear I won't know myself
Fear I won't show myself
Have no reason just this season keep
his reason
Gimmee reason not more treason
To be again for me again
to be again for me again

Like Shards of Glass

Sudden Deceleration Syndrome, (S.D.S)

All I want to do now is sleep
nothing feels as it should
Up means I seem to weep
would stop this if I could
Don't care to bear this dare
face all alone pace all alone
Inside nothing I feel care for
mad ride such thing crash to my core

Feel so tired up so wired down so mired

This despair comes in as a creep
no repair saves the feel as I panic
Now no time to just sleep
like a light switched on I feel manic
Don't care to bear this dare
face all alone pace all alone
Inside nothing I feel care for
mad ride such thing crash to my core

Feel so tired up so wired down so mired

Then sometimes I feel I soar with Eagles
those glad times end lights off I fall less than Beagles
nothing feels as it should
would stop this if I could
Don't care to bear this dare
face all alone pace all alone
Inside nothing I feel care for
mad ride such thing crash to my core

Michael A Budnik

Like Shards of Glass

Numb

Wonder what good feels like?
Something to seek out on a hike?
Sometimes I think I know
take that as chance to grow
It turns out wrong
all alone left reeling
Seems like the same blame song
Guessing wrong takes so long
Does good times ever come?
Bad times I must sever go numb
Good times I did sever all numb
Good times I will sever all numb

To get by some parts have had to die
to see sky no arts can help us try
Sometimes I think I grow
take that as chance to know
It turns out wrong
Guessing wrong takes so long
To get by more parts will have to die
to see sky core parts can help us cry
Guessing wrong takes so long
These bad times I must sever go numb
Now good times I will sever all numb
Now all times I will sever stay numb

To get by core parts will have to die
to see sky no arts can help us try
Sometimes I think I know
take that as chance to grow
It turns out wrong
Guessing wrong takes so long
These bad times I must sever go numb
These good times I will sever all numb
Now all times I will sever stay numb
now all times I will sever stay numb
now all times I will sever stay numb
now all times I will sever stay numb

Michael A Budnik

Like Shards of Glass

Denial

The more I recall those lost times before my fall
The more I know more I just want to lose it all
Must forget this self caught within the wall
Just forget myself must get far 'way from that self
What I don't know must be too bad
What I do know I am so mad
I know this madness must be faced alone
I know this sadness can be erased they have shown
Please let me lose this self no one will miss that self
I cannot face anymore recovered memories
Pain returns all that comes from rediscovered memories

Keep those sad times
cheap those bad crimes
Get away from this self
Cut away from that self
Try to lose what remains
Cry for the loss and all those pains
cry for the loss and all those pains
Try to lose what remains
Cry for the loss and all your pains

Repeat from line 7 in group 1 to end group 2.

Michael A Budnik

Like Shards of Glass

Beyond Redemption

Years I prayed
fears were played
So long I longed for an end
too long "no" song all it would send
Seems this God does not bless
those left in such a mess
No bond exception
beyond redemption

No burning bush
no small voice in the night
telling me to make that push
Telling me I belonged in the light
Seems this God does not bless
those left in such a mess
No bond exception
beyond redemption

No more tears will be shed
to core years have I bled
No burning bush
no small voice in the night
telling me I need to push
Telling me I belonged in the light
Seems this God does not bless
those left in such a mess
No bond exception
beyond redemption

Michael A Budnik

Like Shards of Glass

Measured Response

Subjugation implies negation
back to inflict grieves all relation
Save all your lies wave as all dies
lack of conflict leaves me adrift
Pieces lost as cost in peace's rift
Won't side this ride as will of our nation
Won't buy this guy that claims some gift
You must now go sell what you do so well
Negation belies sublimation

Live in this hate
Must face this fate hope comes too late
No way I can relate
no way I can locate
Give in to hate
give in to hate

Madmen hide within the masses
mad mad mad call now she passes
Show no pity blow some city
Must make it glow just make a show
Lack of conflict leaves me adrift
back to inflict grieves relation
Won't buy some guy that claims some gift
won't side this ride as will of our nation
You must now go sell what you do so well

Live in this hate
Must face this fate hope comes too late
No way I can relate
no way I can locate
Give in to hate
give in to hate
hope comes too late
give in to hate
give in to hate

Michael A Budnik

Like Shards of Glass

Court Jester

Keep tellin' me I'm in good hands
Creep sellin' me hope good guy lands
This lawyer more court jester
Suckin' off some sad cross-dresser
in black like some child molester
Has no concern about the case
I can discern for hope give chase
Seems my future is in the hands
of court jester
Deems my torture must come from stands
of cross-dresser in black child molester

I'd like to change my plea
if this is my best hope
Then for all to see
I flipped off the pope
I must just be a flea

Keep sellin' me hope I'm in good hands
Creep tellin' me the good guy lands
My lawyer more court jester
Suckin' off some mad cross-dresser
in black like some child molester
Has no concern about the case
I can discern for hope give chase
Seems my future is in the hands
of court jester
Deems my torture must come from stands
of cross-dresser in black child molester

I'd like to change my plea
if this is my best hope
then for all to see
I flipped off the pope
I must just be a flea

So get a rope

Michael A Budnik

Like Shards of Glass

Checkbook Justice

Came to this place to seek justice
Tame rage I face for meek justice
I sought it out
they bought it out
Those that wronged
said they wronged
As they just laugh in the face of justice
I'm a castoff from this place of justice

Looks like checkbook justice
The truth is not sought here
a word is just bought here
Sought out restoring dignities
thought not just boring remedies
Crooks like checkbook justice

Those that do harm
have felt no harm
They lose nothing
they use all as nothing
Caught they pay some money
Caught they play some honey
As they just laugh in the face of justice
I'm a castoff from this place of justice

Looks like checkbook justice
a word is just bought here
The truth is not sought here
Sought out restoring dignities
thought not just boring remedies
Crooks like checkbook justice

Michael A Budnik

Like Shards of Glass

Instead of demotions
they head all promotions
None been fired
I'm left tired
Won they say I have it
None will pay so have shit
As they just laugh in the face of justice
I'm a castoff from this place of justice

Repeat fourth group then end

Michael A Budnik

More to Follow

More to follow
found in graves too shallow
More to follow
news so hollow
One tale barely comes to an end
none fail rarely pages without end
News so shallow never fails to notice
Feeds the madness ever nails graves hollow

On the T.V. each day
some nameless soul pay
So there's more to follow
found in graves too shallow
News so hollow
more tears more fears more long to hear
They ride the rating game
as side some mating game

More to follow
found in graves too shallow
More to follow
news so hollow
One tale barely comes to an end
none fail rarely pages without end
News so shallow never fails to notice
feeds the madness ever nails graves hollow

More to follow

Like Shards of Glass

Without Warning

Without warning
the mirror finally fractures
Without warning
the memory lost soul captures

This face I cannot place
must be all the fragments
comin' apart out of their place
or the voices screaming their torments

Without warning
the mirror has lost soul captured
Without warning
the memory lost has fractured

I know my name it stays the same
Years have been lost tears pays as cost
Must be all the broken fragments
or the voices screaming their torments
This face my face I cannot face
comin' apart out of some place

Without warning
the mirror has lost souls captured
Without warning
the memory lost has fractured

Repeat last group

Michael A Budnik

Like Shards of Glass

Like shards of glass
these broken pieces of life
Like shards of glass
these broken lifetimes' memories my life

My shards of glass
can never be made whole again
A mind not so simple won't be whole again
pick up the pieces best you can of your life

Solo

Never a moment without sorrow
but I'll live for the morrow
Some pieces forever lost
and that's just part of the cost

Like shards of glass
these broken pieces of life
Like shards of glass
these broken lifetimes' memories my life

Solo

Michael A Budnik

Like Shards of Glass

Like Shards of Glass

Part Seven

That night you made your choice

Michael A Budnik

Like Shards of Glass

Dancer

She takes the stage
free from her cage
Has golden hair
and such a pair
Here she comes now
to take her bow
she's here to please
not just a tease

She's some dancer
she's your cat-like prancer
no last chance romancer
She's some dancer
she's your cat-like prancer
no last chance romancer
she's your dancer
she's your dancer

She's on the stage
far from her cage
Looks so damn good
just like she knows she should
So take a chance
and then you'll see
she can do more than dance
in much less than a "Gee"

She's some dancer
she's your cat-like prancer
no last chance romancer
She's some dancer
she's your cat-like prancer
no last chance romancer
she's your dancer
she's your dancer

She's off the stage
far from her cage
Looks so damn good
just like she knows she should
So make your chance
and then you'll see
she may do more than dance
in much less than a "Gee"

She's some dancer
she's your cat-like prancer
no last chance romancer
She's some dancer
she's your cat-like prancer
no last chance romancer
she's your dancer
she's your dancer

Michael A Budnik

To Love Again

Must keep my ire
to feed the fire
Let burn that will inspire
to gain that will desire
From nothing will conceive
this nothing will receive

From the ashes they say
a life knew a new day
This land of shades of gray
now rainbow points of ray
You say let go my ire
and just let die the fire

From the dust I can trust
to hold you behold you
Let burn that I inspire
to gain that I desire
Let burn that I desire
to be that I aspire

Like Shards of Glass

Out With the Old

Seems now no matter where I look
love is in the air like a flu
Star-crossed lovers on the hook
someone better comes from the blue
A love turns cold like misty dew

Love is a gift
that can parish
if left to drift
Love we cherish
then love turns cold like misty dew
out with the old in with the new

"Till death do us part" just for the moment
Heart to heart apart more of a torment
Love is a gift
if left to drift
Your love turns cold like misty dew
out with the old in with the new

There is nothin' more I can do
let go this love if you return
Seems now nothin' more I can do
let go your love till you return
Our love turns cold like misty dew
out with the old in with the new

Michael A Budnik

With Regret

I thought I put you behind me
from somewhere you came back and I was wrong I see
Try as I might you I cannot forget
on that last night I came to know regret
That night you made your choice
Damn right I heard your voice

The pain I will never forget
and this chain will break with regret
I know regret wish to forget left with regret

What was done cannot be undone
trust is gone so our time is none
You I know I must now forget
what could be will not be you might regret
This night I make my choice
Damn right you hear my voice

The pain I will never forget
and this chain will break with regret
I know regret wish to forget left with regret

Your touch I still recall
your touch could pass my wall
Try as I might you I cannot forget
what could be will not be you might regret
Damn you you made your choice
Damn you I heard your voice

The pain I will never forget
and this chain will break with regret
I know regret wish to forget left with regret

No One

I think the war maybe over
can never tell
I wonder if I won this one?
This time I fell
was found in a patch of clover
Seems what I fight matters to no one

I wonder will it ever end?
Welcome to Hell
Hell I call home will never send
hope when I fell
'til I can find a better mind
to speak of this place for no one

The war rages
no quarter given or taken
This Hell of ages
can leave those faint of heart shaken
Some would ask why
must this war go on for no one

Welcome to Hell
Hell I call home
Yes it was home where I first fell
it's the Hell I can never tell
No one comes home
War for no one
war for no one
war for no one

Michael A Budnik

Like Shards of Glass

Outrage

By night it screams
pain takes its toll
Try light it dreams
obtain control

It wails
enrage
It rails
outrage

Back I was brought
back to this place
Attack was sought
attack I face
My dreams enrage
my screams of rage
I wail rampage
I rail outrage

My sanity
was left behind
Humanity
cuts like a bind
You want me dear
to face this fear
You run away
Though I must stay

Michael A Budnik

Like Shards of Glass

Stay in the light
obtain control
Day falls to night
pain takes its toll
My sanity
I want to find
Humanity
I lost my mind

It wails
enrage
It rails
outrage

Our sanity
was left behind
Humanity
cuts like a bind
Our sanity
we want to find
Humanity
we lost our mind

Michael A Budnik

Like Shards of Glass

Childs' Play

Bang-bang ha-ha I win
Hey you can get up now
C'mon next time you win
Hey I can show you how

You won't move
don't know what this will prove
We can't play
if you stay down all day

So much red stuff comin'
I think now it's time to call the game
Red stuff I cannot tame
If you don't get up now I'm tellin'

Bang-bang ha-ha I win
Hey you can get up now
C'mon next time you win
Hey I can show you how

You won't move
don't know what this will prove
We can't play
if you stay down all day

Too much red stuff comin'
I think now it's not just our kid game
Red stuff may have a name
If you don't get up now I'm tellin'

You won't move
don't know what this will prove
We can't play
if you stay down all day

We can't play
if you stay down all day
You won't move
don't know what this will prove

Hey you can get up now

Michael A Budnik

Wishing Well

I've been stupid
acted on a feelin'
I've been wishin' to find cupid
acted and I sent you reelin'

Those words spoken
not some token
You wished them from some other
I wished to be that other

So now that's all been left behind
Feelings left crammed inside
a corner of my mind
feelings that I must hide

Now here's a coin for you
and here's a coin for me
All we can do
is wait and see
Toss the coins in
in the wishing well
and be wishing well
yes be wishing well
be wishing well
be wishing well
wishing well

Like Shards of Glass

Mikey's Dead

All I can tell you is what we dread
for so long his life hung by a thread
Mikey's dead! Mikey's dead!! Mikey's dead!!!

It seems so sad
he was too mad
It seems so bad
he was too glad

For too long all alone
that same song now no tone
Mikey's dead! Mikey's dead!! Mikey's dead!!!

He had a choice
he heard a voice
He had a voice
he heard a choice

The reasons this season's last treasons
are between him and God nothin' seen
Mikey's dead! Mikey's dead!! Mikey's dead!!!

All I can tell you is what we dread
for too long his life hung by a thread
Mikey's dead! Mikey's dead!! Mikey's dead!!!

That blame gone now no tone
for so long all alone
Mikey's dead! Mikey's dead!! Mikey's dead!!!

Michael A Budnik

Like Shards of Glass

Play On

A star-gazer said we would meet
though she said your word would be true
A trail-blazer you claim so sweet
I find you feel the sun your due

"Must" the danger "trust" the stranger
Gave you the rope to hang yourself
"Trust" be stranger "must" be danger
Wave to the hope you lost yourself
Wave to the hope you cost yourself
Now with regret play on third fret

On others you count to pay
on mothers you mount you say
You say that your word is true
I say that your word untrue

"Must" be danger "trust" be stranger
Gave you the rope to hang yourself
"Trust" the stranger "must" the danger
Wave to the hope you cost yourself
Wave to the hope you lost yourself
Now with regret play on third fret

Play on Go on Play on
'til it's you they play on
Play on and on and on
'til it's you they play on
Play on Go on Play on
'til it's you they play on
Play on and on and on
'til it's you they play on

Michael A Budnik

www.ingramcontent.com/pod-product-compliance
Lightning Source LLC
Chambersburg PA
CBHW061454040426
42450CB00007B/1348